ROMAN
Myths and Legends

Retold by Anthony Masters

Illustrated by Andrew Skilleter

PETER BEDRICK BOOKS

NEW YORK

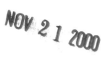

To my mother and father with love, A.M.
To Paul, A.S.

Published in the United States in 1999
by Peter Bedrick Books
A division of NTC/Contemporary
Publishing Group, Inc.
4255 West Touhy Avenue
Lincolnwood (Chicago), Illinois 60646-1975 U.S.A.

Commissioning Editor: Dereen Taylor
Series Editor: Lisa Edwards
Series Design: The Design Works
Book Designer: David Hallas
Production Controller: Carol Titchener

Masters, Anthony, 1940-
Roman myths and legends / retold by Anthony Masters :
illustrated by Andrew Skilleter.
p.   cm.
Summary: A collection of retold Roman Myths, including
those about Did and Aeneas, Janus, and Pomona.
ISBN 0-87226-608-7
1. Mythology, Roman Juvenile literature. [1. Mythology, Roman.]
I. Skilleter Andrew, ill. II. Title.
BL802.M37   2000
292.1'3--dc21   99-25761
CIP

Printed and bound in Portugal by Edições ASA

International Standard Book Number: 0-87226-608-7

99 00 01 02 03 15 14 13 12 11 10 9 8 7 6 5 4 3 2 1

Contents

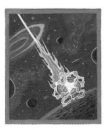

INTRODUCTION

When the Romans conquered the Greeks more than 2,000 years ago, they adopted the gods and goddesses of Greek mythology for themselves, only translating the names into their own language. The Greek god Zeus became the Roman god Jupiter, the Greek goddess Hera became the Roman goddess Juno, and so on. Nevertheless, the stories remain very similar to the Greek originals and are as exciting, mysterious and magical.

Naturally, the Romans added some myths and legends of their own and the five dramatic stories in this book, some better known than others, are all Roman in origin.

In ancient times, these stories helped people to understand the world around them, including how the world was created and what happened to people when they died. This information was chiefly passed around by the spoken word, through the earliest storytellers. The Ancient Greek poets had an imaginative way of describing this process – as if a bird was fluttering from one person's lips to another person's ears.

The reason we are able to enjoy these stories today is because they were passed down through generations of people. They have probably changed much over time, rather like a game where a message is passed from person to person, becoming distorted and getting reinvented each time.

The five Roman myths and legends chosen for this book include the story of Romulus and Remus, brothers whose deadly rivalry ended in murder; Dido, who was reputed to be a witch; Janus, who was born a terrifying monster at the dawn of time; Vertumnus, who adopted the most amazing disguises; and Horatius, who so bravely defended Rome against the Etruscans.

Brooding over each story is the presence of the gods, who, far from being a source of comfort in this ever-changing mythical world, were as unpredictable as life itself.

ANTHONY MASTERS

ROMULUS AND REMUS

The basket bobbed up and down on the fast-flowing River Tiber, threatening to capsize at any moment as the current thrust the flimsy object into the center of the river. Driftwood kept sending the little craft spinning out of control, as it crashed into a floating log and was then sucked out into the center again.

A she-wolf loped along the side of the densely wooded bank and then came to a sudden halt, ears flattened, body crouched. She had heard a thin wailing from the basket. What could be in there? Cubs? It sounded like cubs but somehow the cries seemed different.

ROMULUS AND REMUS, the two babies cast adrift in the basket, were the victims of their great uncle Amulius. Amulius and his brother Numitor jointly ruled over the town of Alba Longa in Italy. But the brothers quarrelled, and as a result Amulius imprisoned Numitor and made his daughter Rhea Silvia a vestal virgin, so that she could never marry and bear a child who might challenge him.

But the gods had other plans. One day, Rhea Silvia encountered Mars, the god of war, while she walked on the banks of the Tiber. As a result, Mars became the father of her twin boys, Romulus and Remus.

Amulius was furious. Determined to wipe out any contenders to

his throne, he had Rhea buried alive, and gave orders that her sons were to be set adrift on the river. But the powerful god of the river floated the baby brothers to safety in their basket, landing them in the shade of a fig tree beside a grotto.

As the she-wolf padded towards the basket, Romulus and Remus stopped crying. They gazed into her green eyes. Being so young and innocent, they were not in the least afraid of her, but only murmured with contentment when she began to lick them gently with her rough tongue. Soon the babies fell asleep.

Later, Romulus and Remus woke and began to cry again, but the protective she-wolf knew exactly what to do. She had raised many litters over the years, and instinctively treated Romulus and Remus as just two more cubs who needed to feed from her milk.

For a while the she-wolf lovingly looked after the boys until they were rescued by none other than the royal shepherd of Alba Longa, Faustulus, who, with his wife Larentia, made them part of their family and brought them up.

Many years later, Romulus and Remus woke one morning to find the sun shining so brightly that the light was almost blinding.

The brothers got out of bed and opened the front door to see a man standing there, the dazzling light radiating from his entire body. He spoke their names slowly and with great love.

"Who are you?" demanded Romulus.

"I'm your father," he replied, "and you are both my beloved sons."

"But you're a god," said Remus, his voice shaking.

"I'm Mars," he explained and began to tell the two young men the story of their birth. It was the first time they had heard it. Mars told Romulus and Remus that it was their duty to take up arms against the evil Amulius and restore their grandfather Numitor to the throne.

After Mars had left, the two brothers were desperate, for they

could never start a revolution on their own. Romulus and Remus lived amongst gentle shepherds and farm-hands who had no weapons or experience of fighting.

Nevertheless, the brothers called a meeting and asked for help. At first the country people were reluctant, but when the shepherds and farm-hands heard how the river god had rescued the boys from the Tiber and how the she-wolf had looked after them, they knew the battle was god-given and willingly agreed to fight.

Armed with only staves and slings, the peasant army marched on Alba Longa and took the inhabitants by surprise. They fought so savagely and with such passion that they soon overcame any resistance. They then sought out Amulius and killed him, restoring the wise law-maker Numitor to the throne.

But their problems weren't yet over. Life in Alba Longa now became so ordered and peaceful that its citizens no longer died violently. Instead, they began to live to a ripe old age. As a result, the place became overcrowded and Romulus and Remus decided to ease the congestion by building a new city. As a permanent memorial to their past, the brothers chose the sacred site on the banks of the Tiber where the river god had rescued them as babies.

Romulus and Remus were more than just brothers; they were close friends as well. But planning the founding of the city was a huge undertaking and it placed a great strain on their relationship. Romulus began to worry that everything was going wrong, while Remus tried to pretend that it wasn't.

One day, while Remus was out hunting with his followers, Romulus marked out the boundaries of the new city by plowing furrows to show where the walls could be built.

But when Remus came home he was immediately jealous of his brother's efforts, knowing that Romulus was giving the plans his full attention and therefore becoming powerful. Remus mocked the new "walls" and jumped over them, laughing and making sure that he humiliated his once dearly loved brother as much as he could.

Romulus was deeply hurt and rivalry broke out between the two brothers, which gradually progressed from teasing to heated arguments.

Romulus now realized he and his brother were not going to be able to rule the new city together. To his horror, he also recognized they were falling out over power, just as Amulius and Numitor had before them. As a result he tried to find a peaceful solution.

The brothers agreed to consult bird omens as to which of them should rule the new city, and they divided the land into two sides, one lucky, the other unlucky.

Remus saw six vultures on the right, which the brothers had decided was to be the lucky side; Romulus saw twelve vultures on the left, which they had decided was to be unlucky.

Unfortunately, they were left with a problem, for they had forgotten to establish which was to be the better omen: more birds on the good side or fewer birds on the bad.

Both brothers argued their own case fiercely, Remus taunting Romulus, goading him mercilessly until his anger spilled over and they began to fight.

The battle was bitter, but for a moment, as they stared into each other's eyes, they almost came to a halt. Then Remus taunted his brother once again, and seizing an advantage, Romulus ran him through with his sword.

Remus sank to the ground covered in blood and Romulus gazed down at him appalled. Kneeling down by his side, he pleaded with the gods to save Remus, but they weren't listening. Remus was dead and Romulus knew he would regret killing him for the rest of his life.

Still grieving, Romulus was made king of the new city which was named Rome in his honor, but he was soon aware that there was a serious drawback: the only citizens were male; no women seemed prepared to live there. It was as if by killing his brother, Romulus had

unleashed a curse against Rome itself. He had to do something, anything, to save his city.

Romulus visited each nearby Italian town and village, inviting their inhabitants to a festival in honor of Neptune, the god of the sea. At the same time, he declared a sacred truce so that friends and enemies could come together safely.

None of the visitors imagined for one moment that a sacred truce would ever be broken, and hundreds of women and children, as well as men, came to the festival. The largest group of all were women from the neighboring Sabine people.

During the festival a number of races were to be run and everyone looked forward to the excitement. Romulus, however, was deeply uneasy for he knew what was about to happen.

Suddenly a signal sounded and the crowds hurried to watch a race between some young Roman men. But just as the race was about to begin the young Romans took out concealed weapons and kidnapped the Sabine women, forcing them to bear their children. Romulus was in despair. But if the truce wasn't broken Rome would no longer exist. The city had to have a population.

But the Sabine men were not going to stand by while their women were kidnapped. They attacked Rome repeatedly and war raged for many years.

Then the Sabine women decided that they had had enough of this men's war, caused by betrayal, power and the desire for revenge. The fighting had to be stopped. The women discussed possible solutions for some time, eventually rejecting each one in turn. But unlike Numitor and Amulius, unlike Romulus and Remus, they didn't argue, for the Sabine women knew that their strength was in unity. Eventually they came up with a plan.

At the height of the fighting, the Sabine women marched shoulder to shoulder between their Roman husbands and the Sabine men and made a declaration. Despite the fact that they had been

kidnapped and forced to bear children, they were now prepared to live with the situation if the fighting stopped. Such was their bravery and so great was their resolution that the war came to an end and a permanent peace was made.

To his intense relief, Romulus discovered the curse had been lifted by the courage of the Sabine women, and for the next forty years he continued to rule over Rome. But the gods had something more in store for him.

Arriving at an athletics festival, Romulus was shown to his throne and was about to declare the games open when he glanced up at the sky and froze. The thickest clouds he had ever seen in his life were hurtling towards him. Yet this was no ordinary storm. The clouds blanketed the arena and Romulus knew that his power, his life and his

grieving had come to an end. He felt himself being lifted from his throne, away from his beloved Rome.

It looked to his people as if he had simply slumped to the ground, dead from a heart attack, but the gods took Romulus's spirit up to Mount Olympus, their own kingdom. There, Romulus was made immortal. Despite his faults, and despite killing his brother Remus, he became the war god Quirinus, follower of his father Mars.

Romulus was worshipped for many centuries as the creator of Rome. After all, he had, by fair means and foul, made sure that the city had survived. Or had he? In his more honest moments, Romulus must have known that the Sabine women, so badly wronged yet so courageous, were the real saviours of Rome.

DIDO AND AENEAS

They watched the witch arrive as they hid behind the sand dunes, peering at the sailing ships bearing down on the North African shore.

Boats had already gone out to greet the strangers. The leader of the expedition was known to be the witch and prophetess Dido who was looking for sanctuary. Her ships carried a treasure that was said to be worth a fortune.

When the fleet grounded in the shallows, dozens of the tribe ran to pull the vessels up the beach. They were anxious to view Dido's treasure, but were equally afraid she might cast a spell upon them. They knew they would have to be extremely careful.

DIDO WAS THE DAUGHTER OF BELUS, KING OF TYRE, and sister of Pygmalion. Unfortunately, Pygmalion killed her husband, Sichaeus, for his wealth and, fearing for her life, Dido was forced to leave Tyre for ever, taking with her as much of Sichaeus's treasure as her ships could carry.

When Dido arrived on the North African shores, she was still in a state of shock. What was more, she had a secret that she hardly dared admit to herself. Dido had the reputation of being a witch, but she knew she couldn't live up to it for long for she wasn't a true sorceress. But she was cunning and determined to survive, so Dido decided to play a trick on the unsuspecting local people.

When they asked Dido what she wanted of them, she humbly asked for "as much land as could be bounded by one bull's hide."

Some of the Africans were pleased that she had asked for so little. Others were suspicious. But when Dido began to cut the hide into strips that were as thin as hairs, the tribe realized she was using cunning rather than magic. They had been conned!

When Dido triumphantly tied the strips together they contained a huge area. She then protected the boundary with so-called magic spells, and with the help of the tribe began to build a vast city which was to be known as Carthage.

Dido was once a member of a powerful ruling family but now all she had was her wealth. She was determined to have power again. She wanted people to fear her, and if she never revealed whether she was magical or not, then she could successfully keep the North Africans guessing.

But the foundations of Carthage had hardly been laid when another fleet of ships approached the sandy shores. Once again the tribe ran down to the sand dunes and, hiding behind them, they watched the fleet anxiously.

Dido strode down to the beach. She looked fierce, but secretly she was afraid that her brother had ordered her assassination. If he had, Dido knew she would have to bribe the tribe into defending her. But the Africans were already working on her new city for low wages, and were almost slave laborers. Dido knew that slaves never made an efficient army.

But instead of being Pygmalion's assassins, the crews were refugees from the war between the Trojans and the Greeks. Amongst their number was a good-looking young man called Aeneas who was the son of Prince Anchises of Troy and Venus, the goddess of love.

Aeneas was brave and dutiful, but that alone wouldn't have been enough for him to survive the fighting in the Trojan War. Many brave and dutiful heroes had been killed, but Aeneas was fortunate; he was protected by the gods.

Neptune, the god of the sea, had made a prophecy: when Troy eventually fell, Aeneas was to lead his people to a new kingdom where they would be able to build their society once more.

Aeneas was proud to be selected, but even with the gods' protection he had only just survived the war. As the invading Greeks had begun to burn Troy, the gods had told Aeneas to commandeer a fleet of ships and to take as many survivors on board as possible, including his wife, his son and his frail old father. Aeneas had then been told to sail due south and find a new home.

Aeneas had a huge responsibility in sailing through uncharted waters and making landings in hostile countries. The survivors he was taking with him could easily be drowned or killed. He also had a mystical task to fulfil – a task, however, that might give him and his crews even more supernatural protection. Aeneas had to take with him on his voyage of destiny the sacred images of the gods and found a second and greater Troy. He could not have been given a more important job. The future of his people rested entirely in his hands.

After surviving many adventures, the sea had almost defeated the expedition when Juno, queen of the gods, sent a violent storm, hoping to destroy the fleet. Juno still found it impossible to forget that she had been slighted by another Trojan—Paris, Prince of Troy. As a result, Juno decided to defy the gods and exact her revenge upon Aeneas.

Looking up, Aeneas had seen the thunder clouds gathering and lightning beginning to flicker. For the first time in his life he had felt as if he had lost control. Could this be his ultimate test?

With a huge clap of thunder, the heavens had opened with driving rain and the terrible sound of a raging hurricane that had begun to scream in the rigging of the fleet.

The waves had become enormous as the ships had been driven off course, heading towards the North African coast. The helmsmen had lost control and the storm had threatened to overwhelm the fleet, particularly as some of the ships were now heading for the rocks.

Furious at the interference of Juno, who was acting without his permission, Neptune had raised his head above the waves in rage, watching Aeneas's fleet driving before the gale.

Neptune had calmed the rolling waves and had then brushed away the clouds from the face of the sun. He had pried some of the fleet off the rocks with his trident while his son, Triton, had set still more of the ships afloat again with the help of a sea nymph.

Now that the storm was over, the battered fleet was seeking sanctuary on the coast near Carthage, Dido's city in the making.

When she saw the windswept figures of Aeneas and his crew, as well as the badly damaged ships, Dido was both horrified and deeply relieved. At least her life wasn't in danger and these men had not come as assassins; she had nothing to fear.

Badly shaken by their experience, Aeneas and his fellow survivors jumped down on to the beach to be welcomed by Dido, her followers and slaves.

She received the heroic exiles with great warmth and told Aeneas, "Not unacquainted with distress, I have learned to help other people in trouble." Aeneas was relieved. He badly needed rest, safety and a chance to get his confidence back.

When Aeneas and his men had rested, Dido laid on a huge display of hospitality. She was desperate to keep the survivors in Carthage for she had fallen in love with Aeneas.

Seeking to impress him, she organized games of strength and skill between her followers and the Trojans. These went well and both sides began to trust each other. Close friendships began to spring up.

Then Dido generously proclaimed that winning the games was unimportant. All she wanted was unity between her followers and the

Trojans and particularly between her and Aeneas.

Far from rejecting Dido, Aeneas seemed delighted at first. His wife had been lost in the confusion of their escape from Troy and Aeneas had to shoulder the heavy burden of responsibility for everyone. Now he felt he could afford to fall in love again.

After the games, he sat with Dido, giving her a full account of the fall of Troy and his own magical adventures. As he talked, she became even more consumed with love for Aeneas, a love that was possessive, that would stop at nothing to own him.

Dido wanted Aeneas to rule Carthage with her and defend the city against its neighbors, who were gradually getting jealous of her ambitions. The land she now owned was still a vast building site, but it promised to become a very powerful city indeed.

To Dido's joy, Aeneas seemed to want to settle down and to accept a home, a kingdom and a new bride.

Months passed and Aeneas and Dido's love grew. They could think of no one else – or nothing else – but each other. As a result, no progress towards completing the city of Carthage was made.

The gods were furious for they found this kind of selfishness quite intolerable. Dido had a city to build and Aeneas a destiny to fulfill, but like many weak human beings, they were so locked into their love for each other that they had completely forgotten they had a duty to found new civilizations.

So Jupiter dispatched Mercury with a message. With a chill of dismay, Dido saw the

winged figure of the messenger of the gods speed like an arrow to Aeneas. She was sure that Mercury had come to separate her from Aeneas, that he was deliberately splitting them up and ruining her life. Dido was right. Jupiter's message was all too clear: Aeneas had to resume his voyage immediately and to remember that he had a higher cause to serve than falling in love with Dido.

Aeneas went to Dido and told her what she had already half guessed. But she couldn't agree to let him go. All she wanted was Aeneas to be hers for the rest of their lives. She pleaded desperately, but Aeneas had now remembered his duty. He was resolute and wouldn't listen. Of course, he could see how bitterly miserable she was, but his destiny and that of his followers now seemed far more important than Dido's love for him – or the love he had had for her.

The ships repaired, his men fit, well and inspired again, Aeneas set sail while the tormented Dido gave her own instructions. She demanded that a funeral pyre should be erected in a place prominent enough for Aeneas to see as his fleet sailed from Carthage.

Terrified but not daring to disobey her, Dido's followers built the pyre. Holding aloft a knife, Dido gazed out to sea, wanting to punish Aeneas in the worst way she could. Hoping he would know she was about to take her own life, Dido plunged the knife into her heart and then jumped into the flames of her funeral pyre.

From the bridge of his ship, Aeneas saw the fire rising over Carthage and guessed what had happened. But despite his grief he knew he couldn't let Dido's suicide prevent him from fulfilling the destiny of his people. After many adventures he successfully guided them to Italy, where, at Alba Longa, his descendant, Romulus, eventually founded Rome.

JANUS

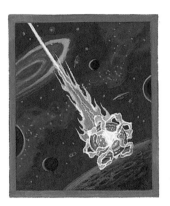

Chaos was coming — a living organism whirling through the planetary system, made of fire and light, turning over and over in the heavens like a meteorite.

But Chaos was alive and was bringing life to a planet that hadn't yet been properly formed. The planet was called Earth.

When the living organism crash landed, Uranus, or Father Sky as he was sometimes known, was the first of two beings to emerge.

Uranus stood looking at the huge and desolate planet that was as lifeless as the moon. There were mountain ranges and valleys, plateaus and plains, but none had life, only dust and rock.

Uranus's first task was to summon life-giving rain, which poured from his outstretched hands, watering the arid land, making the planet green and fertile.

Then Gaia, Mother Earth herself, emerged from Chaos and gave the planet life, forming the oceans and rivers and creating plants and animals that began to inhabit the land and sea.

EVIL WAS NEVER FAR BEHIND GOOD, THOUGH, and it landed on Earth in the dark shape of Hecate, goddess of black magic, who was also the queen of ghosts. Hecate was deeply feared, even in the Underworld, which was her domain.

Whip in hand, she would dance across the Underworld, a pack of ghosts screaming at her heels, sometimes emerging into the upper world to be seen lurking at lonely crossroads, usually at midnight.

Hecate was also a moon goddess and mortals could sometimes see her serpent body galloping across the sky, holding a torch that had a strange, unearthly light. Perhaps it was because of this more romantic part of her character that Uranus fell in love with Hecate. He decided to offer her a gift and knew that her darker side, as the goddess of black magic, would be delighted by something very unusual.

Uranus thought over his gift for a long time. What would really attract Hecate? What would make her eternally grateful to him? What might make her love him?

Then Uranus had an inspiration. He would give Hecate a child. Uranus knew that she had always dreamed of having one and, of course, Father Sky would be able to create a special son for her.

Taking equal portions of earth, air, water and darkness, he molded them into the shape of a ball and rolled his present through a crack in the Earth's crust that led straight down into the dark regions of the Underworld and to Hecate's lair.

Uranus also knew that the descent of his gift through the Underworld would give his creation a magical life of its own.

As the ball rolled down to the Underworld it changed shape and became a long pillar, turning over and over, the friction of the fall transforming the inanimate object into a living creature. The thing was already beginning to move and make sounds for itself, a baby monster that needed nursing.

Hecate had a strong mothering instinct and to Uranus's delight she was deeply grateful for his gift. To nurture her monstrous son, she wrapped him in her own coils and provided a diet she thought would nourish the infant. The Underworld menu included woodlice, fresh from under a log, warm lamb's blood and the entrails of young dogs. Hecate called her adopted baby-monster Janus.

The revolting diet and the howling of Hecate's ghostly servants made Janus afraid. He began to grow increasingly restless, to hate his adoptive mother and long for freedom.

Snuggled up in her coils, munching on entrails and woodlice, drinking warm lamb's blood was more like a preparation for eternal hell than life. And it was life – ordinary life – that Janus wanted. But to achieve his ambition he knew he had to escape from his demonic mother and he began to plan.

Hecate had no idea how much her adopted child-monster hated and was repelled by her, for she had never been so happy or fulfilled. Looking after a baby was so much more rewarding than being trailed by howling banshees or hanging around at crossroads. But Janus was already plotting his escape. All he needed was the right opportunity.

One day, when Hecate was otherwise engaged in rounding up her flock of ghosts, the infant Janus took his chance and ran, plunging into the Styx, the main river of the Underworld. The freezing waters carried Janus to the upper world, washing him up on the banks of the River Eridanus in Italy.

As he lay exhausted, the sun rose and began to warm Janus's body. Earthly light was just what he needed and he began to grow. But Uranus had not given him a human shape and the sun only produced a scattering of recognizable features.

Janus grew too many heads and legs and arms, ears and eyes and noses. He was hideous – at least to mortals. Hecate had loved Janus in the Underworld but in the upper world no one loved him at all; everyone regarded him as the terrifying monster that he resembled.

24

Seeking to hide his deformity, Janus ran through the countryside for more than seven centuries, lurking in the densest of woods, hiding himself in thickets and long grass. If anyone did discover him, they would run screaming from the spot. So he sought sanctuary in caves and dark places, trying to avoid meeting anyone at all. Now Janus was as lonely as his mother had been.

Janus often thought of Hecate. She might have had some strange habits, she might have given him revolting things to eat and drink, but at least she had loved Janus and cuddled him up in her coils. He almost longed for his demonic mother.

One day, a young shepherd found him asleep under an oak tree in a forest. The boy stared at the monster's many ears and eyes and legs and arms and his body that looked something like a pillar with many heads. For some reason his curiosity overcame his fear and the boy remained motionless.

Janus opened one eye – and then all the others in all the other heads – and he and the young boy gazed at each other, transfixed.

"Who are you?" the young shepherd asked.

"I'm Janus."

"Why are you so different from me?"

"I don't know," Janus replied. "I was made as a present for Hecate."

The boy froze at the mention of the goddess of black magic. She was much feared on Earth and many people worshiped her in the hope that she would leave them alone.

The shepherd boy's parents often laid out offerings for Hecate in the form of corn, milk and wild bees' honey. They had also told him about the sacrifices that were laid at the feet of guardian statues placed wherever three roads met – the dreaded crossroads where Hecate and her ghosts would lurk. Each statue had a serpent's body and neck, but with three different faces – those of a horse, lion and dog.

The shepherd boy remembered all too well that the sacrifices included newborn lambs and puppies. He mentioned the fact to Janus

who immediately replied, "Hecate made me eat the entrails and drink the warm blood. Maybe that's why I look the way I do."

But rather than running away from Janus in disgust, the shepherd boy felt desperately sorry for him, realizing the monster was forced to hide out in thickets and forests because he was so hideous.

"I'll be your friend," said the boy, offering his hand.

Janus grabbed it with one of his many arms. He had never felt so grateful and was immediately filled with hope.

The shepherd boy ran home and spread the word about Janus.

His next visitor was the boy's mother who brought him homemade food and drink. Gradually other visitors came over and began to treat the monstrous Janus like a friend.

Soon, because they suspected he had magical gifts, the local people began to worship him as a god, but Janus didn't want this; after centuries of loneliness he just needed friends. These he made in abundance and Janus lived in peace in Italy for many years, no longer feeling forced to hide himself away. He was accepted, despite his appearance.

But then a battle began between the gods, the offspring of the Titans, and the Titans themselves for control over the Earth. At its height, Saturn, the leader of the Titans and half-brother to Janus, was forced to find sanctuary in Italy.

Angry with the Italians for sheltering one of their enemies, the gods began to hurl thunderbolts at the country, killing a large number of people and demanding to know where Saturn was hidden.

Janus was beside himself with anxiety. If he didn't reveal Saturn's hiding place, hundreds more citizens would die. But if he did reveal where he was hiding, then he would be betraying his half-brother. In the end he decided to insist on a condition: If the gods promised to show Saturn mercy, then Janus would reveal his hiding place.

The gods kept to the bargain and exiled the Titans to the Islands of the Blessed, but Jupiter, the king of the gods, himself elected to deal with Janus. The decision came as a shock to everyone and particularly to Janus. He was to be rewarded for giving away Saturn, but also punished for helping his half-brother find sanctuary in Italy.

Janus was terrified. Was he going to be dispatched to some isolated place where his loneliness would begin all over again? Or, worse still, sent back to Hecate in the Underworld?

Jupiter, however, had a very specific task for Janus.

He made him a god and sent him to Mount Olympus, but appointed him the doorkeeper of Heaven. Janus was to be in charge of the single moment of time when the old year dies and the new year is born.

Janus was rooted to the spot, looking like the pillar he so closely resembled, but now with only two heads. One of his faces gazed rigidly ahead and the other stared just as fixedly behind.

Janus had become immortal, but although he had a task, he knew all too well it was a worthless one. And sadly, what Janus had feared most had come true. He was alone.

POMONA

Pomona was being watched. She lived in an orchard near the River Tiber, and although she was very beautiful she was so busy tending her apple trees that she had no time for any suitors at all.

But Vertumnus, the god of orchards, was determined to put a stop to all that and he was now hiding behind a tree, wondering how he could make Pomona notice him. He kept trying to gather the courage to come out and talk to her, but he lost his nerve every time.

Vertumnus knew that if she saw him he would be ordered out of the orchard and told never to return.

As he was deeply in love with her, that was the last thing Vertumnus wanted. But how could he make Pomona love him?

VERTUMNUS SOUGHT THE ADVICE OF PALES, the goddess of pastures. She advised him that the answer lay in the very skill that Vertumnus brought so regularly to his own work. Each autumn, his duty was to turn the leaves on the trees from green to gold and make sure they floated down to the ground so that in the spring new ones would grow in their place.

"You can change the leaves in autumn from green to gold," Pales explained to Vertumnus patiently, "so why don't you change yourself from shy to bold?"

But Vertumnus was not able to alter his personality so easily. He knew he just couldn't do it. So what was he going to do? He was besotted with Pomona and loved her more each day. He couldn't sleep because of his because of his love and knew that he would die of a broken heart if he didn't make Pomona notice him somehow.

Then Vertumnus had a brainwave. Why not change himself completely? Why not wear a disguise?

Coming from a long family line of wood nymphs, Pomona had no interest in rivers, seas or mountains. She was simply devoted to her orchard. Armed with her knife, Pomona made sure the apples did not grow too densely, cutting the branches that straggled out of place. Pomona also took care that her apple trees didn't suffer from drought and diverted streams so that their thirsty roots could drink.

The trees were her only passion; she had never encountered Venus, the goddess of love, and as a consequence she had no interest in men whatsoever. In fact she was afraid of them.

In the past, Pomona had had many suitors including Pan, who was the god of shepherds and flocks. He was always trying to entice her from the orchard, but Pomona rebuffed him, turning away in disgust, knowing her pruning knife was her protection.

But Pan still persisted, and one afternoon Pomona saw him hovering yet again. She sighed as she worked on her trees. Would Pan never give up?

He stood watching her. From the waist down he had a goat's body. From the waist up he looked like a man but with a goat's ears and horns. He often played his pan-pipes for Pomona, and from time to time he would give a loud shout, so loud that it had been known to split castles in two and send whole armies into retreat.

But Pan's bellows couldn't reach Pomona. Her apple trees rustled mockingly, deflecting the sound. They weren't afraid of Pan.

Pomona, however, was still wary of him and felt that men, even if they happened to be half goat, were an aggressive nuisance.

"Go away, Pan," she cried.

He shouted at her even louder and a gale raced through the trees. But none of the apples fell. Pomona loved them far too much to allow that; her protection was their strength.

She watched Pan run back to his home – the woods and water meadows – to be greeted by his subjects, the satyrs, who were also half human and half goat. Pomona laughed mockingly and Pan waved a fist at her threateningly. He was furious.

Vertumnus, meanwhile, had been watching his rival with interest, noting how crude his approach had been. He wasn't going to make the same mistake as Pan. Vertumnus was going to try to appear before Pomona in an acceptable disguise – a disguise that was designed to appeal to her gentle nature. He would have to think very carefully and come up with a disguise that was going to work.

Vertumnus decided to experiment. He first disguised himself as a reaper, someone who was gentle and a lover of nature. Wearing a belt of twisted hay, he brought Pomona corn in a basket, but although she allowed the disguised Vertumnus into the orchard, she showed not the slightest interest in him.

Vertumnus then tried another disguise, this time appearing as a rugged farmer. But Pomona still ignored him.

Beginning to panic, Vertumnus then impersonated someone who tended the vines, complete with a pruning hook. When this role made no impression he hastily came up with a swift succession of other disguises: an apple-gatherer carrying a ladder over his shoulders, a soldier, a fisherman and a bee keeper. But still she seemed completely uninterested. The only consolation was that at least he had got nearer to Pomona and kept his love for her alive.

Vertumnus knew, however, that he would have to take a different approach if he was to make her notice him. He racked his brain for something really clever. Then he had another idea.

Vertumnus appeared in the orchard dressed as a sweet old lady, with grey hair under a cap and a staff in her hand. She admired the fruit and Pomona, always kind and helpful to women, particularly if they were old, made her welcome.

The old lady gazed around her, admiring the fruit. "All this does do you credit, my dear," she said warmly. "What a hard worker you are." Impulsively she kissed Pomona.

If Pomona was a little surprised at the strength of the kiss she didn't show it. Instead, she returned to her work as the old lady sat down on a bank and looked up at the overhanging branches laden with fruit. Opposite was an elm entwined with a vine hung with swelling grapes which gave Vertumnus an idea.

Taking care to continue speaking in what he hoped was an old lady's voice, Vertumnus said wonderingly, "If that tree stood alone and had no vine clinging to it, there would only be useless leaves. But together they've both achieved a good deal more."

He glanced at Pomona but she was hardly listening, absorbed in her pruning as she was. Vertumnus raised his old lady's voice, speaking more forcefully.

"And if the vine wasn't twisted round the elm, it would simply lie on the ground and bear no fruit."

He watched Pomona, but she still didn't seem to be listening. Vertumnus's old-lady's voice was getting shrill now. "Why don't you take a lesson from the tree and the vine, Pomona? Why don't you unite yourself with someone?"

"I've no need to," she replied quietly, snipping away. "I have my fruit."

Vertumnus became more desperate still

and decided to take an even greater risk.

"Why don't you let an old woman advise you? Accept Vertumnus as your suitor – on my recommendation. I know him as well as he knows himself. He's not like most lovers these days, who love everyone they see. Vertumnus only loves you. He's young, handsome and can disguise himself. He also likes doing the same things as you do. For instance he really loves gardening, particularly in orchards, particularly growing apples."

Pomona shrugged, still concentrating on her pruning, yawning slightly, as if the old lady was beginning to bore her. Vertumnus wondered if she was listening at all.

He had to do much more than this to get through to her, so he decided to give Pomona a more gripping example of what he was trying to tell her. Vertumnus began to tell a tragic love story.

"Iphis was a young man of humble background who had fallen in love with Anaxarete who was the daughter of a noble. He knew he stood no chance, but in the end Iphis became so obsessed with Anaxarete that he arrived at her house and pleaded with her nurse and servants to speak up for him. Quite understandably they couldn't help, so Iphis went to even further extremes and started writing to Anaxarete on tablets of stone as well as hanging garlands at her gate. But she only mocked Iphis and uttered cruel words of rejection.

"Weeping, he turned away from Anaxarete's house, fastened a rope to the gatepost on which he had previously hung garlands, and putting his head into the noose cried out, "Here's one garland that should please you!"

"He fell and hung suspended with a broken neck, dying at once.

"Anaxarete's servants found him, and feeling desperately sorry about his frustrated love and his untimely death, carried Iphis home to his mother.

"Days later, the mournful funeral procession slowly paraded through the town with Iphis's corpse carried on a bier towards his

burial place. By chance, Anaxarete's house was on the route that the procession passed, and hearing the weeping of the mourners she ran to the window.

"As soon as she saw Iphis's corpse, Anaxarete began to stiffen and the warm blood in her body froze. Trying to step back, away from the window and out of sight of the funeral procession, Anaxarete found that she couldn't move. By degrees, all her limbs became as stony as her heart.

"Anaxarete had become a statue and was moved to the temple of Venus at Salamis where she still stands."

When Vertumnus finished his story there was still no sign that Pomona had listened to any of it. She seemed to be totally engrossed in a rather delicate piece of pruning and she didn't even turn round.

In desperation, Vertumnus stood up and threw off his disguise as the old lady, becoming again the handsome youth that he really was. Still Pomona didn't notice him.

Vertumnus spoke angrily and with considerable bitterness. "Why don't you consider what I've just told you? Think about poor Iphis and cold, cold Anaxarete. Lay aside your scorn. Accept my love."

Still Pomona showed no sign of hearing, and somehow managing to be patient and calm Vertumnus repeated his plea.

But she didn't even bother to turn round and look at him. Snip went her scissors, as if she were cutting Vertumnus out of her life.

He got up and turned his back on her, feeling as suicidal as Iphis had and wondering if he should follow his example at once. After all, although he was young, what was the point of life without Pomona?

Vertumnus walked slowly towards the gate of the orchard which was high enough to hang himself from. If only he could find some rope. How come Iphis had such a convenient supply? Had he brought it with him, just in case?

Vertumnus suddenly turned, as if by instinct, and saw to his amazement that Pomona had stopped her incessant pruning and was

staring after him.

They stood transfixed, gazing into each other's eyes.

Pomona looked bewildered, as if she was trying to work something out. Then, as she stared at Vertumnus even more intently, her expression changed to sudden joy.

"You're beautiful," Pomona said, as if she had just seen a vision.

"More than an apple tree?" he demanded.

She nodded and began to run towards him, arms outstretched.

Vertumnus did the same and they met half way, in the middle of the orchard, the trees rustling over their heads.

Pomona and Vertumnus spent the rest of their lives together, deeply in love, working in the orchard, harvesting crop after crop of apples as they tended the trees.

HORATIUS

Horatius, Lartius and Herminius had stationed themselves at the head of the bridge. In front of them stood the invading Etruscans, hoping to seize the city of Rome. Behind them was the Roman army, trying to cut the bridge down.

Below ran the swiftly flowing River Tiber, spanned by a single wooden crossing. If the three young soldiers couldn't hold the Etruscans off until the bridge was demolished, the city of Rome would fall and the invasion would be complete.

Slowly the Etruscans drew nearer, their faces wreathed in contemptuous smiles. What could three puny Roman soldiers do to save their city? The Etruscans would kill them in a few seconds.

Wiping away the sweat and trying to keep his nerve, Horatius wondered how long the three of them would be able to hold out. More importantly, how fast could the Roman army cut down the bridge?

LARS PORSENA, THE COMMANDER OF THE ETRUSCANS, paused before he gave instructions for his army to mow down the three young Roman soldiers. He had never seen such bravery. Then Porsena realized his hesitation could be fatal, for the Romans had already cut half way through the timbers of the narrow bridge.

"If you don't move away," said Lars Porsena to Horatius, Lartius and Herminius, "we'll kill you."

"Just try!" yelled Horatius, raising his sword.

Porsena gave his Etruscans the order to attack.

Both Horatius and Porsena, however, knew that the Etruscans had a slight advantage over the Romans. The bridge was very narrow and Horatius and his two comrades would only have to face three Etruscan soldiers at once. However, even if they killed the first three soldiers they would be quickly replaced by another three. Each trio of new opponents would be fresher and more alert but Horatius and his comrades would be getting more and more exhausted.

Knowing the first wave of soldiers would attack at any moment, Horatius looked back over his shoulder and yelled at the Roman commander, "How's it going, sir?"

"We won't be long." The commander's voice rang out over the welcome sound of sawing. "The timbers are tough but we'll get through them. Do your best. May the gods be with you."

Horatius, Lartius and Herminius fought the first three Etruscan soldiers under a blinding sun, the clash of steel echoing around them. But the Romans were not forced back and soon killed their opponents, piercing their heavy armor with their swords.

As their next opponents appeared, Horatius again glanced back, yelling at the Roman commander, "Haven't you finished yet?"

"The timbers are thick," he replied grimly.

"How long?"

"We're doing our best."

The cutting down of the bridge seemed to be taking a very long time and already Horatius was exhausted, his heart hammering, his breath coming in gasps. But at least he hadn't been wounded yet and neither had Herminius or Lartius.

"How long?" he shouted desperately once again. "Just tell me how long?"

"Only seconds now," came the reply. "Only seconds."

Horatius knew he couldn't hold out much longer, knew his strength was draining away.

"Yield," shouted Lars Porsena to the Romans. "Yield now."

But Horatius, Lartius and Herminius simply fought on.

Then, suddenly, Horatius could feel a juddering and a vibrating under his feet and realized with incredible relief that the Roman army had succeeded in cutting down the bridge. The piles began to topple and Horatius yelled at Lartius and Herminius to escape, to jump back to the Roman side of the river. They hesitated and he continued to shout at them, still holding off an Etruscan swordsman.

As the last timbers of the bridge were severed, Lartius and Herminius ran back, and Horatius plunged his sword through the armor of his opponent, who fell into the Tiber.

He was alone now on what was left of the bridge, with the enemy in front of him and the river behind. He could see the rest of the bridge being swept away in the torrent and knew there was no way he could get back to the Roman side without swimming across the Tiber. For a moment he hesitated and so did the Etruscan army. Several men had their hands on their swords but they were all looking to Lars Porsena for direction, just as they had before the fighting began. One thing was clear: with Lartius and Herminius on the other side of the river, it would be all too easy to rush at Horatius and kill him.

Still Lars Porsena hesitated.

The Romans looked on from the other bank of the river. They knew that Horatius had to jump off the ruined bridge.

"Yield," said Lars Porsena again. "Surrender to us now."

Horatius glanced back and was sure he could see the white porch of his home glinting in the sun on Palatinus, the most central of the seven Roman hills. He was going home. Horatius jumped.

"Take charge of me," he whispered to the god of the river.

Horatius tumbled over and over before hitting the surface with a mighty splash. Complete with sword and heavy armor he disappeared underwater, being pulled down so deep that he thought he would never come up again.

On both banks, the Etruscan and Roman armies watched in silence, gazing at the spot where Horatius had sunk. Then both sides gave a spontaneous cry of joy as Horatius suddenly surfaced; but he was swept on by the current which was swollen by months of rain.

He struggled, sank and then rose again, weighed down by his armour and the stiffness of his bruised body. But just as they thought they had finally lost him, the Romans saw Horatius rise to the surface again, battling the current, heading downstream, striking out for the bank that was Rome.

The Romans gazed at Horatius intently, praying that he would survive. They sank to their knees and prayed while the Etruscans watched; the Etruscans felt a reluctant concern for their gallant foe.

Horatius sank yet again and on this occasion he disappeared for a long time. A great groan went up from the Roman bank. Had the

Tiber ignored their prayers? Then cheering rang out as Horatius surfaced again, striking out feebly for the riverbank.

Again the Romans knelt in prayer to the river god, but it was Lars Porsena who saw that one of the bridge timbers wedged against the bank had broken loose. The block of wood was now viciously coursing its way down the torrent, turning in circles, straight towards the struggling Horatius.

Involuntarily, Porsena called out a warning and his cry was taken up on both banks, the two armies shouting in unison, trying to make their voices heard above the roaring of the Tiber.

But still Horatius did not look back, nor did he hear the great cry from either bank. He was simply concentrating on keeping his head above water and not being pulled back into the center of the river by the current.

Horatius swam on towards the landing stage, each stroke a mighty effort, until he heard a faint noise that he was sure couldn't be the sound of the Tiber. He glanced over to the Etruscan ranks and saw that they were pointing at something in the water. Then he gazed up at the nearer Roman bank and saw that his own army was doing the same.

Above the torrent he heard something strike the bank behind him with a terrifying thump and, looking back, saw the huge piece of broken timber from the bridge bearing down on him in the current. Covered in foam, it lashed through the waves, swinging viciously to and fro.

Summoning up his last shred of strength, Horatius dived deep beneath the surface of the water, turning over on his back and seeing the dim shape of the timber dark above him, like a river monster. He heard a dull, underwater clunking sound and then, seeing the shape disappear, clawed his way back to the surface, his lungs almost bursting for air.

As Horatius's head emerged, another great cheer went up from

both sides of the Tiber, but he barely heard the sound. To his horror, bearing down on him, spinning round and round in the sunlit water, was yet another huge piece of timber.

He had to get to the broken jetty fast.

Striking out to the cheers of both armies, Horatius swam a last few desperate strokes, feeling a sudden and miraculous second wind as if the river god were really listening now, guiding him towards the shore. Then a rush of water pushed him forward and to his intense relief his feet found the bottom.

Hundreds of Roman soldiers were running towards him, grabbing his hands, dragging him up the bank and lifting Horatius high on to their shoulders while the Etruscan ranks gave a last cheer from the opposite shore.

The soldiers took Horatius through the River Gate of Rome where a vast crowd surrounded him, shouting, clapping and weeping aloud. Horatius had saved the city along with Lartius and Herminius; the Etruscans would never take Rome now. As a reward, Horatius was given land and oxen and the grateful Romans also made a statue of him that stood by the river for centuries.

When he had recovered a little, Horatius went to the banks of the Tiber and prayed. The armies had gone and the level of the river had dropped. The water flowed more quietly now, peaceful in the twilight. All that was left of the bridge was two stumps of timber on each shore.

Horatius began to walk back through the streets of Rome, heading for the Palatine Hill. All the while as he made his journey he was greeted as a hero. Soon, however, he was free of the crowds and bounding up the springy green grass of the hillside. He had never been so happy.

"The hero has come home," whispered a shepherd boy, herding his sheep into night pasture. Horatius began to run towards the light shining in his porch.

People and Places in Roman Myths and Legends

ALBA LONGA A town in Italy, about 12 miles from Rome, which was founded by the son of Aeneas (see ANCHISES/DIDO).

AMULIUS Joint ruler of Alba Longa with his brother Numitor. He was in charge of the army and imprisoned his brother, taking control of the city.

ANCHISES The Prince of Troy, who was considered to be the most handsome human being ever born. Venus, the goddess of love, admired him and bore him a son: the hero Aeneas. When Aeneas escaped from the siege of Troy, he carried his much-loved father to safety on his own shoulders.

CARTHAGE This city was built to the north east of modern Tunis in North Africa. It was founded by Dido when she fled from her brother Pygmalion, King of Tyre.

DIDO Founder of the city of Carthage. Dido and her lover Aeneas had one final meeting after he had abandoned her and she had killed herself. When Aeneas visited the Underworld, he saw Dido in the shadows, wandering sadly amongst those who had died of love. He tried to say he was sorry and explain why he had had to go, pleading with Dido to speak to him. But she turned away and passed Aeneas by in silence.

ETRUSCANS People who lived on the west coast of Italy many years before the city of Rome was founded. They were very powerful, but after many battles they were defeated by the Romans in 300 BC.

MARS The god of war and son of Jupiter and Juno, the king and queen of the gods.

MOUNT OLYMPUS A mountain in northern Greece, believed to be the home of the gods. The Ancient Greeks, from whom the Romans adopted this belief, believed that this was the exact center of the world.

NEPTUNE The brother of Jupiter and Pluto. Between them, they ruled over heaven (Jupiter), the sea (Neptune) and the Underworld (Pluto).

NUMITOR The joint ruler of Alba Longa with his brother Amulius. He was in charge of the administration of the town and its people.

PALATINE HILL/PALATINUS One of the Seven Hills upon which Rome was built. The Roman emperor's palace was situated here along with the homes of wealthy Romans.

PARIS The son of King Priam of Troy. The night before he was born, his mother dreamed that she gave birth to a torch whose flames would burn the city of Troy to the ground. As a result, the baby was left on a hillside to die but he was saved by a she-bear and lived a simple life as a shepherd. However, when there was an argument between the goddesses Venus, Minerva and Juno as to which of them was the most beautiful, Jupiter gave the task of making the decision to Paris. Each of the three goddesses tried to bribe him, but in the end he selected Venus. As a result, she offered him the most beautiful woman in the world, but unfortunately this was Helen of Sparta, who was already married. When Paris took Helen to Troy, her husband and his warriors destroyed the city. Paris's mother's dream had come true.

PYGMALION The son of Belus, King of Tyre and brother to Dido, founder of the city of Carthage.

RIVER TIBER The river that runs through Rome, the Tiber was named after King Tiberinus of Alba Longa. When the king drowned in its waters, Jupiter made him the god of the river.

SABINE PEOPLE An ancient tribe who lived in the mountains east of Rome's River Tiber.

TITANS Gigantic in stature, these were the first human beings to be created by Chaos, god of the unformed Earth. The gods and goddesses of Roman mythology were the children of the Titans.

TROJAN WAR A legendary war between the Greeks and the people of Troy that lasted for ten years. The Greek poet Homer told the story of the war in his poem the *Iliad*.

TYRE An ancient city of Phoenicia (modern Lebanon), known for its extreme beauty.

UNDERWORLD In Roman mythology, the place filled with the spirits of dead mortals. Some were being punished for sins against the gods; others lived more peacefully in happier surroundings. Occasionally the living were allowed to pass through on a mission. The Underworld was also filled with demons, giants and monsters who had opposed the gods and were busy producing creatures even more unpleasant than themselves.

VESTAL VIRGINS Priestesses who tended the sacred fire in the temple dedicated to Vesta, goddess of the family hearth. They were not allowed to marry or have children.

INDEX